SIX WEST WARWICK

COMPILED & PUBLISHED BY WOOTT
GROUP © 200

CW01574408

INTRODUCTION

In this, the fifth walks guide that Wootton Wawen Footpaths Group has produced in its 30-year existence, our aim is still to suggest pleasant circular walks in the Warwickshire countryside. Typically, these take about five hours to complete, including a lunchtime stop, but options are given for those who prefer shorter walks.

Most walkers currently have to use their cars to reach the start of a country walk, which does little to help the environment that they are out to enjoy. So our walks are centred on six stations along the North Warwickshire railway line, which provides easy access from many parts of the Birmingham area – see Train Service on page 4. If you still prefer to travel by car, details of parking places are given in the text.

Conditions on public paths in much of Warwickshire have improved in recent years. Our routes are now waymarked along most of their length. Mud is an inevitable hazard that may be encountered on any of the walks, especially during the winter months; Warwickshire clay has a particularly glutinous quality! See our note on Clothing and Footwear on page 27.

Although legislation should ensure that farmers reinstate ploughed paths and do not obstruct them with arable crops, there may be times when paths are less convenient to use than they should be. Under- and overgrowth can be a problem in summertime and some stiles are not user-friendly. It is the duty of Warwickshire County Council to ensure that all its public paths can be used and enjoyed by all, and the reporting of problems, initially to this group at the address on page 19, can help the highway authority to perform that duty effectively.

Having mentioned possible difficulties, we must emphasise that, with proper preparations, you should complete your walk with a feeling of well-being and achievement.

Every care has been taken to ensure the accuracy of this booklet, but the compilers cannot accept responsibility for injury, damage or other misfortune suffered as a result of its use. Particular care should be taken when using canal-side paths and roads without footways. In the latter case, always walk so as to face the oncoming traffic.

ACKNOWLEDGEMENTS

The printing of this booklet was largely financed by a National Lotteries Charity Board grant under its Millennium Festival Awards For All scheme.

Help and advice were received from the Countryside Access team of Warwickshire County Council and from Central Trains Ltd, Birmingham.

Text by Denis Keyte
Maps by Ron Holmes
Design and word processing by Judith Wright
Cover photographs by Denis Keyte

FRONT COVER: Wootton Wawen Footpaths Group walk round Earlswood Lakes in August 1999.

BACK COVER: Class 150 trains at Wootton Wawen and Henley-in-Arden stations.

THE WALKS IN BRIEF

1. **EARLSWOOD LAKES** There are no hills on this 7 mile walk or its 4½ mile alternative. Much of the route is alongside water or in woodland. There is a choice of four refreshment places.

2. **WOOD END & TANWORTH IN ARDEN** A well waymarked route that crosses and recrosses both the North Warwickshire railway and the youthful River Alne. The main walk is a little over 7½ miles long, and the shorter option 4½ miles.

3. **DANZEY & ULLENHALL** At 5¼ miles, or 4¼ miles for the alternative, this is not a taxing walk. Watch out for Pig Trot Lane, Perry Mill Lane, and other road names that evoke memories of the area's rural past.

4. **HENLEY-IN-ARDEN & CLAVERDON** A 7½ mile walk, easily shortened by three miles, with some gradients to tackle and views to admire from the high ground in Claverdon. Well provided with refreshment opportunities.

5. **WOOTTON WAWEN & BEARLEY** At 8½ miles, this is our longest walk, but there are 7 and 5½ mile alternatives. Austy Wood is attractive, especially at bluebell time. There is some walking along quiet roads, needing care.

6. **WILMCOTE & ASTON CANTLOW** A 7 or 4½ mile route that encircles the site of the old Wilmcote quarrying industry. The 100 ft difference in level between the two villages is evident on the ground. *Not recommended in the rainy season.*

TRAIN AND BUS SERVICES

In 2000, there was a basic hourly service on the North Warwickshire line. On Sundays, trains stopped at only three of our suggested starting points – The Lakes, Henley-in-Arden, and Wilmcote.

The Stratford to Birmingham (Moor Street and Snow Hill) route was also served by many through trains to Stourbridge Junction, thus providing an easy journey from several north Birmingham stations. Passengers from the Solihull area could travel on the Leamington to Birmingham line, but the connection with the North Warwickshire line service needed careful checking. It should be noted that those entitled to travel concessions in the West Midlands cannot use their passes beyond the limit of the Centro area at Earlswood.

For up-to-date information, please see the time-tables at your local station, or call the Centro enquiry line on 0121 200 2700, or Warwickshire Traveline on 01926 414140.

In 2000, there was a basic hourly bus service (X20) on the Birmingham (New Street) to Stratford route, but with a much reduced frequency on Sundays in winter. The starting points of the Henley and Wootton Wawen walks can be reached by this means. Time-table details are available from Warwickshire Traveline or the Centro enquiry line – see above.

MAPS

Our sketch-maps should be adequate for confirming the description of the walks, but they will not enable the more ambitious walker to vary the routes or to appreciate the general topography of the area. For that, Ordnance Survey 'Explorer' maps at 1:25,000 scale should be used. Number 220 (Birmingham) covers our Walks 1 to 5, and number 205 (Stratford upon Avon) covers nearly all of Walk 6.

WALK 1

EARLSWOOD LAKES

If you arrive at the The Lakes by train, turn left out of the station along Malthouse Lane, then left again after 120 yards, down Cloweswood Lane. Continue to the end, where a kissing gate leads to a grassy path to a stile near the west end of Terry's Pool.

Car users will find a public car park further along Malthouse Lane. The access is on the north-west side of the road, near a telephone box. Please refer to the final paragraph of this description for details of the route from the car park to the stile mentioned above.

Use the stile, and head for the railway level crossing which is slightly hidden in the trees on the right. After the crossing, aim for the stile in the corner of the next, long, meadow. For the next mile or so, the marked way does not strictly follow the legal route, but it keeps just outside Clowes Wood – a site of special scientific interest – all the way round to the railway footbridge. After the bridge, turn right to keep near the fence. The official path ahead is obstructed, so about 50 yards after passing a railway level crossing it is necessary to bear left, through an open area. Descend into mature woodland, where you cross another path and a tiny bridge. Soon, cross two bridges and then keep right at any junctions of the tracks through the holly-rich woodland. After nearly 400 yards, you should reach the fisherman's path round Terry's Pool. Turn left, and enjoy the much-improved surface of the lakeside path.

The lakes were formed nearly 200 years ago as a reservoir to feed the Stratford Canal. You can view two of the 'pools' from the walkway and causeway between Terry's Pool and the Engine Pool – we see Windmill Pool towards the end of the walk. Do not cross the causeway, but continue on the path round the edge of the Engine Pool, which forms the boundary between Warwickshire and Solihull. Just past the Engine House, which in 1999 was due for restoration, we join the road at a rather hazardous spot – please take care. *THIS IS THE POINT AT WHICH IT HAS TO BE DECIDED WHETHER TO TAKE THE SHORTER ROUTE. IF SO, TURN RIGHT AND GO ALONG THE WHOLE LENGTH OF THE DAM TO A GATED PATH ALONGSIDE WINDMILL POOL, AND IGNORE THE NEXT TWO PARAGRAPHS.*

The longer route turns left, over the narrow road bridge, and then right at the nearby crossroads. Keep to the right of the Red Lion public house, and continue along Lady Lane for 650 yards. Join the towpath of the Stratford Canal, heading east, past moored narrow-boats. The feeder canal from the Engine Pool joins the main canal 100 yards or so from the road.

Leave the towpath after about a mile, at the third bridge, near the Blue Bell public house. Head back, parallel to the canal, along Lime Kiln Lane. Turn right at the T-junction by the Bull's Head public house, and then left into Shutt Lane. After half a mile, we reach the cross-roads, with our fourth place of refreshment in 2½ miles – the Reservoir Hotel – on the corner. Turn right at the crossroads, and then take the minor road that forks to the left, up to the corner of Windmill Pool.

The path alongside the pool can be muddy at times; maybe it will be improved. At the south-east corner, turn right along a public path – also liable to be muddy – that joins a track leading to Malthouse Lane. Turn right along the road for 150 yards, where a signed path, just before a telephone box, goes past the car park that we mentioned in our second paragraph.

The path reaches Terry's Pool and turns left to follow the water's edge to the western end of the pool. The stile over the bridge is the finishing point of the route for rail travellers; they will now have to retrace their steps to The Lakes station.

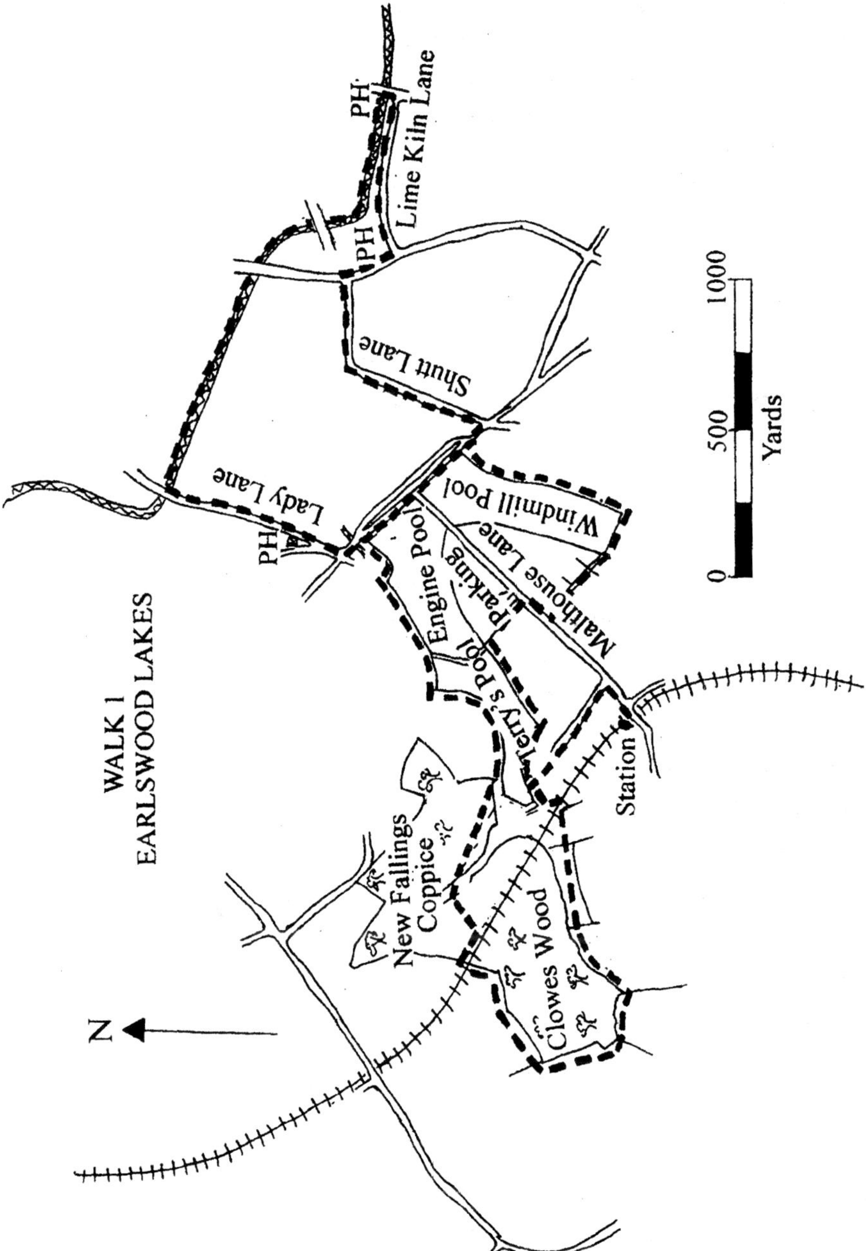
WALK 1
EARLSWOOD LAKES
PH
Lime Kiln Lane
PH
Shutt Lane
Lady Lane
PH
Windmill Pool
Engine Pool
Parking
Malthouse Lane
Terry's Pool
Station
New Fallings Coppice
Clowes Wood
N
0
500
1000
Yards

WALK 2

WOOD END & TANWORTH-IN-ARDEN

The lay-by on the B4010 road outside the access to Wood End station should provide limited parking.

Head up the road for 150 yards, where our path starts opposite the Old Royal Oak; it soon descends between fences to a stile. Continue (with Tanworth church ahead) to near the bottom corner of the field, and cross the railway line with care. Follow the railway fence for 100 yards, where the bridge over the River Alne will be seen. After crossing that, be careful to use the left-hand of the two stiles in the nearby fence, and continue up the field to another stile in the top left-hand corner. Then carry on down, to reach the road at a stile in the corner of the field.

NOW THERE IS AN OPPORTUNITY TO SHORTEN THE WALK BY 3½ MILES BY FOLLOWING THE ROAD UP TO THE GREEN, AND IGNORING THE NEXT THREE PARAGRAPHS.

Otherwise, cross the road to follow the avenue of balsam poplars that line the way to the Children's Farm. The railway bridge over this road is noteworthy: The land owner in the early 1900's made its elaborate stone construction a condition for allowing the line to pass over his land. Where the road turns off to the Children's Farm, we continue up the sometimes muddy track to complete the 1½ mile dead straight part of our route. Near the top, pause to admire the view over the Avon valley and the Cotswolds beyond.

Have a look at the late 17th century Umberslade Hall when you reach the road, then head right along it for 600 yards. Opposite the lodge, a field path follows the edge of the first field, and curves round the boundary of the second to a rather concealed bridge. Then we pass through a young plantation, and 100 yards after that, reach a junction of paths. Here we turn right and

WALK 2
WOOD END & TANWORTH-IN-ARDEN

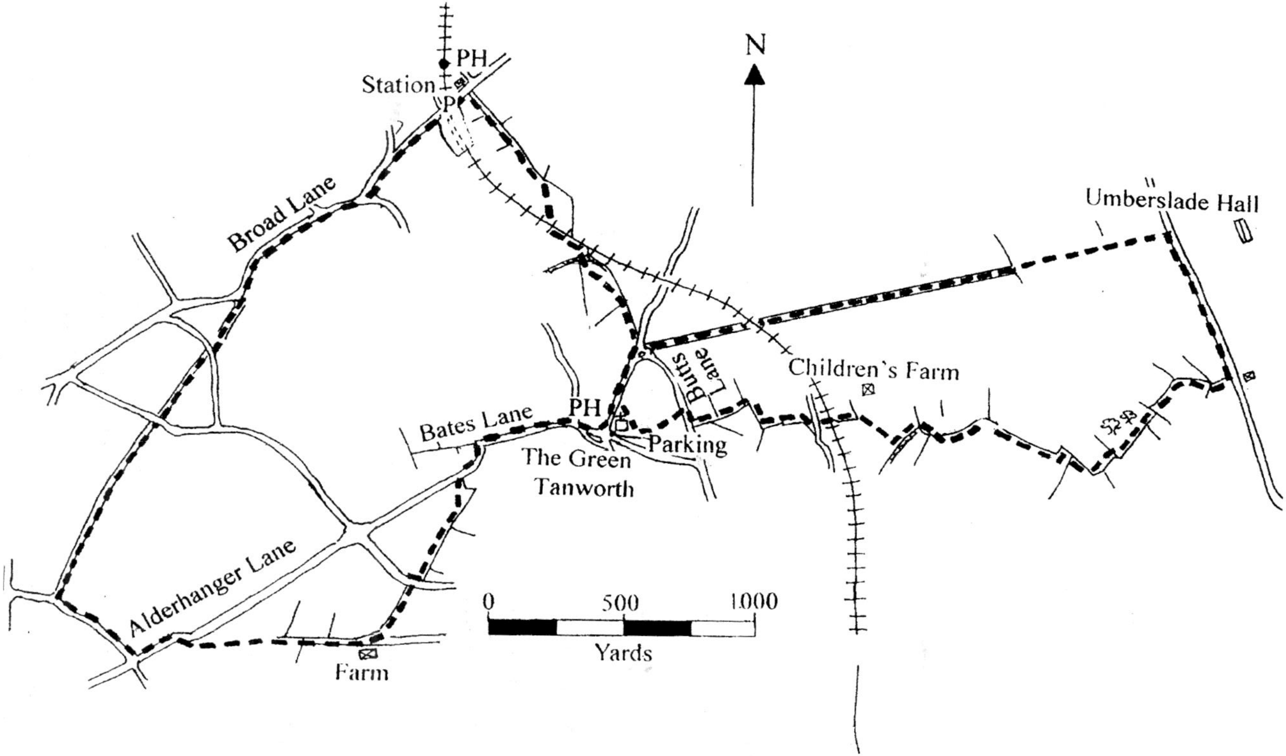

follow the northern boundaries of fields for nearly half a mile. At a field corner, with the Children's Farm just 300 yards away, go through two waymarked field gates into a meadow dotted with old oak trees. Officially, one should go left along its boundary for 100 yards, before heading directly away from the stream to reach the track to a railway bridge, near the most westerly of the oak trees.

After passing under the railway, cross the next field to make the second crossing of the River Alne. Then go clockwise round the edge of the field ahead for 300 yards before crossing into a young plantation; the well-worn path continues to Butts Lane. Forty yards up the lane, head up the field into the churchyard, and reach The Green by going to the right of the church.

You may wish to pause to admire the largely unspoilt village centre, and perhaps visit the Bell Inn or the village shop.

Walk to the end of The Green and along Bates Lane. Descend the hill after the left-hand bend, and climb the stile on the left, just past the Tanworth-in-Arden sign. Follow the hedge to farm buildings and pass between two barns to emerge on a lane.

Go right for 60 yards, where the field path continues. After passing a barn, it joins a bridleway by Oakwood Farm. Turn right, and continue along the bridleway for 700 yards where it meets Alderhanger Lane. Turn left along the lane, following it round to the right after 250 yards. You will eventually be within sight of the busy A435 road, but 200 yards before reaching it, take the track on the right. This continues, virtually straight, for nearly a mile, crossing a couple of roads, before joining Broad Lane for the last ¾ mile of the route. However, there is a long-standing drainage problem on the bridleway between the second road crossing and Broad Lane. Until this is resolved, be prepared to retreat, and use Aspley Heath Lane to join the main road somewhat further away from Wood End.

WALK 3

DANZEY & ULLENHALL

On leaving Danzey station car park, turn left, and soon after crossing the railway bridge take the bridleway on the right. On re-crossing the railway, you may admire the quality of the bridge, which is typical of the North Warwickshire line. 150 yards after the bridge, use the middle gate and follow the hedge on the right. The track curves, eventually heading north, but at the junction of four hedges it turns left, along the boundaries of two fields, to reach a lane at Forde Hall Farm.

Go briefly left along the lane, then turn right, between farm buildings, with the usual paraphernalia of a modern working farm. The path continues along the boundaries of two fields. At the end of the second, now planted with trees, turn left for 100 yards, with Little Forde Hall on the right. After crossing the stream turn left, to follow the right-hand boundary of the field along what was evidently a tree-lined lane many years ago. This crosses a stream and continues for nearly half a mile. It may be overgrown, in which case there may be a better path along the edge of the cultivated field. On reaching Forde Hall Lane again, turn right and soon pass Mockley Manor residential home.

The lane leads directly to Ullenhall (¾ mile), but a more interesting way and our shorter route that avoids the centre of the village start at the stile on the left-hand side of the road some 50 yards past Mockley Manor. It passes in front of the buildings, through three fields, after which it follows a substantial hedge on the right, descending to a stile. Cross the meadow ahead, keeping parallel with the left-hand boundary, and reach the road at a T-junction.

OUR SHORTER ROUTE FOLLOWS THE ROAD (GENTLEMAN'S LANE) TO THE LEFT FOR 400 YARDS. THEN GO STRAIGHT OVER THE GRASSY TRIANGLE AT THE ROAD JUNCTION TO A STILE, RATHER CONCEALED IN

THE HEDGE. CONTINUE THROUGH THREE FIELDS, EVENTUALLY FOLLOWING THE HEDGE BORDERING WHITE PUMP LANE. A STILE LEADS ONTO THE LANE JUST A FEW YARDS FROM THE 3-WAY ROAD JUNCTION WHERE THE MAIN ROUTE IS REJOINED – SEE THREE PARAGRAPHS BELOW.

The main route continues along Perry Mill Lane (sign-posted Ullenhall ¼ mile). After 400 yards, just after The Old Thatch, look for a stile on the right. That leads to a bridge, after which we keep to the left-hand field boundary and follow the path between gardens to the road, where a left turn soon brings one to the village street. The Winged Spur inn is 250 yards down the road.

From the pub, continue down the main street, but soon go to the left of the war memorial to Watery Lane. Go left, but almost immediately take the path up on the right. After a gate, this curves round farm buildings and heads up a meadow, near the right-hand hedge. It crosses a lane and continues up the middle of the next field, reaching a road junction where we maintain the same heading along Chapel Lane. After a couple of hundred yards, go up the 'no through road' to St Mary's Chapel.

Our path turns left near the top of the road, but a slight de-tour to walk through the churchyard, with good views from the far side, can be recommended. Resume the route at a stile near the row of restored cottages, first following the hedge on the right and then the line of oaks, to the field corner at the three-way road junction. Here, the shorter alternative way rejoins the main route.

Use the waymarked field gate at the road junction, keeping the garden and paddock fences on the left and then continuing to a not-too-obvious stile and bridge in the hedge on the left. Head up the long narrow meadow to a stile in the right-hand corner. The next field has paths following all its boundaries; we go clock-wise to its tapered end, where a stile leads into a paddock, with the railway level crossing nearby.

After the crossing, aim away from the railway at an angle of about 45° to the left, to pass close to the end of an isolated

Walk 3
DANZEY & ULLENHALL

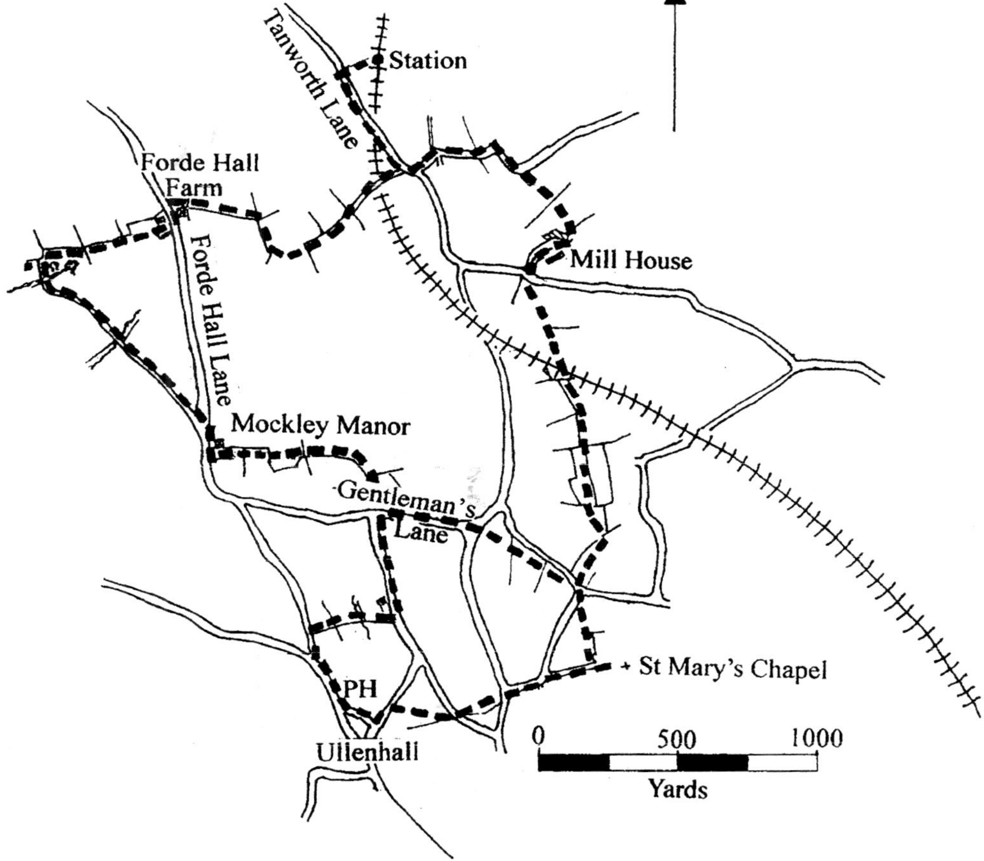

hedge, and continue across the meadow to its bottom left-hand corner. Cross the road to the drive to the Mill House, where the mill pond and site of the water-wheel are still visible. The water-mill was in use until the beginning of the second world war. The site of Danzey windmill is reached by following the path to the left after the (probably empty) pond, to a stile into the next field. The only evidence of the windmill is a mound in the field some 60 yards from the stile. The structure was removed in the 1960's to Avoncroft Museum, where it was restored to working order.

Our path passes just to the left of the mound, to a gap in the hedge at the top of the hill. Now there is a track down to a sometimes muddy gateway onto the lane. Follow that to the left for 500 yards, where a right turn along Tanworth Lane soon brings one back to Danzey station.

WHY THE NORTH WARWICKSHIRE LINE?

Even though Birmingham was part of Warwickshire when the line between Tyseley and Bearley was built in the early 1900's, there seems to be no justification for calling it the North Warwickshire Line; geographically, it's the West Warwickshire line. The only explanation, suggested by John Boynton in his book 'Shakespeare's Railways', is that the line ran through the territory of the North Warwickshire hunt!

WALK 4

HENLEY-IN-ARDEN & CLAVERDON

There are several ways from Henley station to the High Street; the most direct footpath starts almost opposite the station bridge and will take you to within sight of St John's Church and within easy reach of a variety of pubs, restaurants, and cafes. The X20 bus stop is at the A3400/Station Road junction.

The walk to Claverdon starts along Beaudesert (with the accent on the second syllable!) Lane, which adjoins the church. A second church – St Nicholas's, dating from the 12th century – is soon seen. Parking restrictions are likely to be introduced here, but Henley's main car park, with access from the Warwick Road, is only a few minutes' walk from Beaudesert Lane if the pedestrian way over the river bridge is used. Note that market traffic makes use of the car park difficult on Wednesdays.

From the end of Beaudesert Lane, use the kissing gate and climb the steep slope ahead. The public path uses the shoulder below and to the left of the summit of Beaudesert Mount before continuing across the valley on a beaten track, to reach the top corner by power lines.

Here, the Heart of England Way goes on ahead, but we turn right over a stile by the electricity pole and follow the hedge for 200 yards to a gate. With your back to the gate, aim half-right for a stile on the lane to Kite Green.

Go along the twisting lane, through the hamlet. Just after the isolated white cottage (Kate's Cottage), enter the field on the right, keeping the hedge on the left. Cross into the next field in the corner, and immediately cross the stile under the old pear tree to head across towards the right of farm buildings. The way

continues over three stiles and passes close to the timber-framed Church Farm before reaching the road in Preston Bagot.

Over the road, a path climbs up to Preston church – a good viewpoint. Keep in the meadow in front of the church, and reach Preston Fields Lane by the car park.

Almost opposite, the path continues at right angles to the lane. After a gateway, turn to keep the hedge on your right to the bottom of the field. After another stile, a roundabout way takes one over the river and to a bridge adjoining Lock 36 of the Stratford canal.

TO SHORTEN THE WALK BY 3 MILES, USE THE CANAL TOWPATH TOWARDS THE LOCK COTTAGE. AFTER 450 YARDS, JUST PAST A WHITE-PAINTED CANALSIDE BUNGALOW, YOU REACH THE 'COURSE OF THE OLD ROAD' REFERRED TO SIX PARAGRAPHS BELOW.

Use the waymarked field gate by the bridge to go along the canalside field boundary. Pass through a little thicket on the Preston/Claverdon boundary and then, as the canal curves away, keep on the same heading – over marshy ground – up to the far corner of the field. From there, go half-right, up the slope with a hedge on the left, through two fields and along a track on Yarningale Common.

On meeting the tarmac road, turn right down the gravel track, past the old chapel. Go left after the kennels to enter fields, first with the hedge on the right and then on the left. Head at an angle across the third field and after crossing Hercules Lane continue along another old lane, much improved in 1999, though it could still be muddy.

After 120 yards, look for the way over the stream into a long narrow field on the right. Go along its length to a stile in the top right-hand corner, where a narrow track leads to Lye Green Road in Claverdon. A roadside car park opposite enables motorists to start the walk from here if they wish.

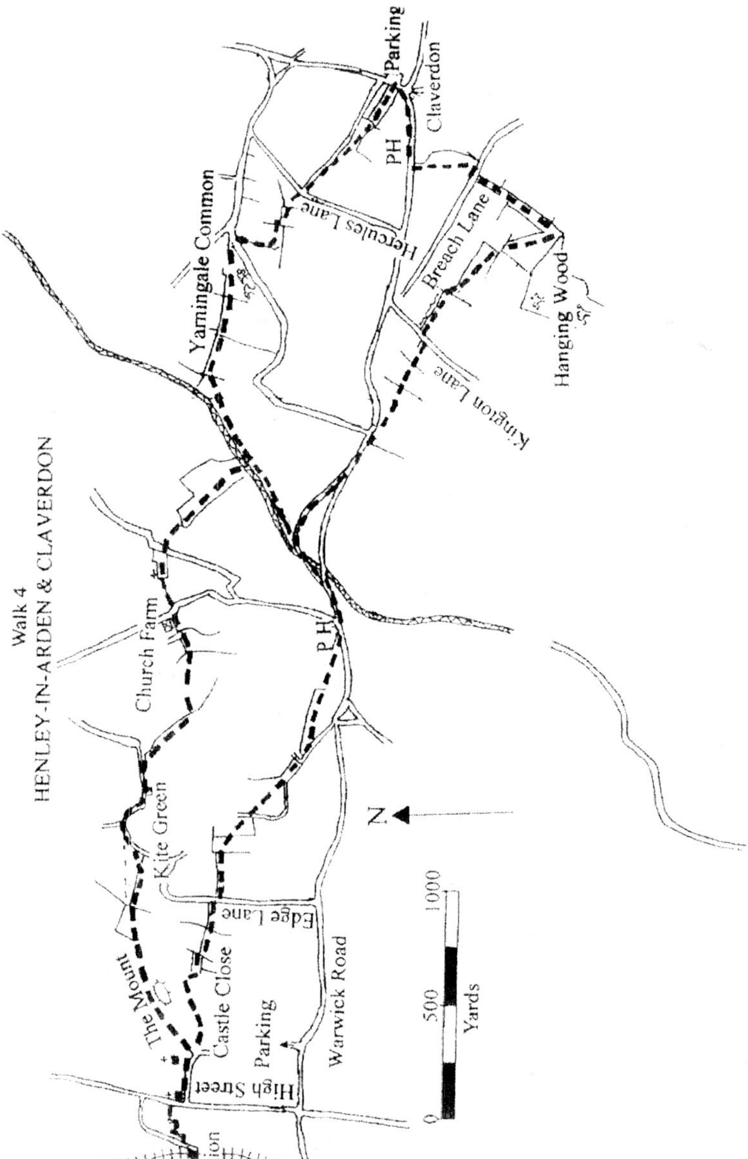
Walk 4
HENLEY-IN-ARDEN & CLAVERDON
Parking
Claverdon
PH
Yarningale Common
Hercules Lane
Breach Lane
Hanging Wood
Kington Lane
Church Farm
PH
N
Kite Green
Edge Lane
The Mount
Castle Close
Parking
Warwick Road
High Street
Station
0
500
1000
Yards

Set off past the shops and turn right at the A4189 Warwick to Redditch road. A little way past the Crown Inn, on the opposite side of the road, a path goes near the left-hand edge of a meadow. By the top corner, a stile leads to another old track – Breach Lane. Turn right and, after 50 yards, left alongside the wall that protects the converted buildings – a far cry from the original Breach Farm! Continue along the ridge to the corner of the narrow extension of Hanging Wood, noted for its bluebells.

Do not enter the wood, but turn through more than a right angle to follow a fence diagonally down the grassy slope. After the stile at the bottom, turn right briefly, enter the next field to go diagonally across it, to a barn along the far boundary. A stile behind the barn brings you into a rough field with industrial buildings on the left. Make your way anticlockwise round the boundary, ignoring the drive to the buildings, and continue between gardens and the stream to emerge on Kington Lane. Thirty yards to the left, the path continues through a thicket, over a stile, and straight up the field ahead to a gate. Maintain the heading to the corner of the next field and reach the A4189 again. Cross that road to go leftwards for a couple of hundred yards.

Although one can continue along the verge of the rather busy road, it is more pleasant to use the course of the old road that curves past the white-painted bungalow before rejoining the main road. There, turn right towards the Crab Mill Inn.

Enter the field immediately after the inn, keeping the short length of hedge on the right. Maintain the same heading to cross a stile, then keep the hedge on the right, ignoring the gate halfway along. In the top corner of the field, cross onto the lane to Preston Green.

Go to the right along the lane. Ignore branches to left and right, but continue straight ahead for 600 yards. That will take you through a field gate, then across in turn a meadow (aim about halfway along the opposite hedge), a hedged track, and two more fields before turning half-left at the junction of field boundaries. Then follow the hedge on the right to Edge Lane.

Almost opposite, the path continues, still with a hedge on the right. After 120 yards, it transfers briefly to the other side of the hedge before descending by steps to the residential area of Beaudesert. It crosses Castle Close, goes round school playing fields, passes the top of Meadow Road, and reaches the end of Beaudesert Lane.

The way back from the High Street to the station may be varied by turning left at St John's church and using Beck's Croft, opposite the Nags Head.

WOOTTON WAWEN FOOTPATHS GROUP

The group was formed in 1970 to encourage the proper use of public paths in and around the village. Apart from publishing walks guides, its main activity is the organisation of a monthly walk of about five miles in the local area. These take place on the last Sundays of January to November, and on 26 December, leaving Wootton village hall at 2.15 p.m.

In 2000, the members of the group were Deborah Brown, Ron Holmes (treasurer), Denis Keyte (secretary), Mayou McCall, Ernie Shuttleworth, David Steele, and Judith Wright. These are in effect the committee of an organisation that has no formal membership, and charges no fees. All are welcome to join in its activities!

Reports of any problems encountered when using this booklet should be sent to the secretary at 'Sunnybank', Wootton Wawen, Warwickshire, B95 6BH.
Tel. 01564 792872

WALK 5

WOOTTON WAWEN & BEARLEY

On the 600-yard way from Wootton station to the A3400 road through the village, you will pass the Bull's Head inn and the village hall. One or two cars can usually be parked behind the hall without difficulty. St Peter's church, the oldest in Warwickshire, overlooks the main road and the village stores, with the bus stop from Birmingham opposite.

The route to Pennyford Lane via the lane opposite the gates of Wootton Hall was in 2000 often muddy and in part squalid, so we suggest continuing down the A3400 (with a good view of the Hall) and using the path on the right, just after the Waterfall Bridge. 100 yards after the cattle grid, turn half-left to the plantation near the far corner of the field. A gate through the conifers leads to Pennyford Lane. Go right for 120 yards, then up the track to the canal.

To omit the Austy Wood and Cutlers Farm section of the walk, and to shorten it by 3 miles, turn right along the canal towpath to the Edstone aqueduct and resume the main route there.

After crossing the canal bridge, turn left along the canal bank, then right at the group of poplar trees. Continue up a slight depression in the field, over a stile, and on, through two field gates, to reach the A3400 again, opposite the drive to Austy Manor.

Follow the footway to the right for 250 yards, then cross the road to the handsome double gates into what was Austy Wood. Much of the wood was cleared in the 1970's, so now, after the narrow strip of replanted woodland, our path heads along the length of a usually arable field. If the path is not obvious, keep about midway between the hedge on the right and the conifers on

WALK 5
WOOTTON WAWEN & BEARLEY

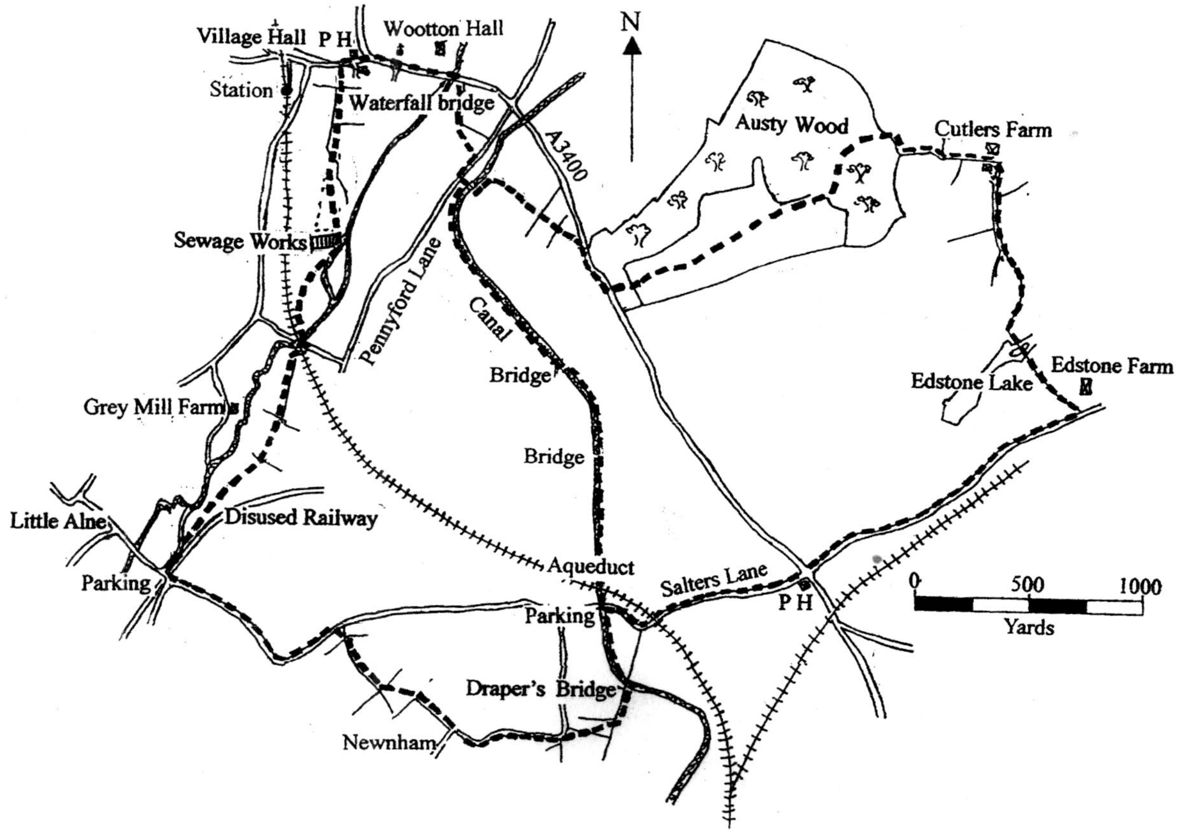

the left for 600 yards, then head for the far left-hand corner of the field, where our path enters the mature woodland. Its course through the trees is indicated by tapes and waymarks. You may notice an area on the left that was planted in the mid-1980's with oak, larch, and southern beech (nothofagus). The growth of the latter has been remarkable.

The woodland path joins a bridleway and soon leaves the wood at a gate. Follow the edge of the next field anticlockwise to the bottom of the steep slope, then continue along the track to Cutlers Farm, now converted to business use. Turn right along the drive and follow that (turning left before Edstone lake) for nearly a mile to the Langley road by Edstone Farm.

A right turn and ¾-mile of road walking brings one to the A3400 cross-roads and the Golden Cross inn. Continue along Salters Lane for half a mile. Beware of traffic, as the verges of this road may be overgrown in places. After passing under the railway, the impressive aqueduct, dating from 1813, comes into view. Use the steps to reach the canal, and maybe admire the view from above the railway.

To omit the Newnham and Little Alne section of the walk, and shorten it by 1½ miles, cross the aqueduct and continue northwards along the towpath to the third bridge (by Pennyford Lane) and retrace your steps to the village centre.

Our main route goes south along the towpath for quarter of a mile to Drapers Bridge, which we cross. Go across the corner of the field ahead, to follow its right-hand edge for 200 yards before crossing into a meadow. The path goes diagonally, via a stile, to emerge at a bend in the lane to Newnham.

Follow the lane to and through the hamlet. Soon after the tarmac road turns into a bridleway, a path starts at a field gate on the right. Follow the hedge for 200 yards, then turn half-left to cross the next field to a stile. Then with the hedge (good for

blackberries) on the left, we proceed to Salters Lane, near Whitehouse Farm. Go past the farmhouse and keep on the road for over half a mile. Just after the T-junction to Aston Cantlow, we cross the route of the old railway to Alcester and then immediately on the right (waymarked as a footpath) a county 'E-road' starts. This curves to the left at the bottom of the slope and soon a field path starts at a stile on the right.

The path goes through a new plantation to a bridge on the Aston Cantlow/Wootton Wawen boundary. It continues ahead, parallel with the river on the left. If a dry way across the ditch in this field cannot be found, go towards the river to find a convenient crossing point; then resume the original heading to a sometimes muddy gateway into the next field. There, follow the flimsy fence almost to its end, then turn right to go under the Pennyford railway bridge and over the River Alne.

The route home continues, officially between the two railway fences alongside the concrete road to the sewage works. At the end of this enclosed path, it veers across the meadow to the right-hand corner of the sewage works fence, which it then follows for 250 yards.

At the end of the works, a waymark may indicate that the official path goes to the left, but for more than 35 years walkers have gone straight across the field ahead, to join the tree-fringed ditch. This soon peters out, and the path transfers to the other side of the hedge, in a boggy field where the course of the River Alne once ran. Two more stiles take one to The Dale and the village centre.

WALK 6

WILMCOTE & ASTON CANTLOW

Wilmcote station is a convenient point from which to set off on this walk, but those travelling by road may not find roadside parking in the village easy; they might consider starting the circular walk in Aston Cantlow instead. See the note on parking at the end of Paragraph 5 below.

From Wilmcote station, turn left at the road and pass the canal and Mary Arden's House before turning right by the Mary Arden Hotel into Aston Cantlow Road. Here you will find the Post Office Stores, the Mason's Arms, and the Men's Club. Opposite the latter is a track 'Foxes Lane' that leads into a field, where we turn right and continue along a well-used path for over half a mile before reaching Marsh Road via a sometimes muddy paddock.

Turn right briefly along the lane before resuming the westerly heading along a fenced path. With a few twists and turns, and good views ahead, this descends the scarp. At the bottom, cross the (usually arable) field, then turn right, go through a gateway, and keep the hedge on your left until you reach the Aston Cantlow Road again.

HERE IS YOUR CHANCE TO SHORTEN THE WALK BY 2½ MILES: TURN RIGHT AT THE ROAD. AFTER 100 YARDS, USE THE BRIDLEWAY UP THE SLOPE, THROUGH THE END OF THE BELT OF TREES, AND ON, EVENTUALLY PASSING ABOVE THE OLD QUARRY FACE. THEN IT CONTINUES WITH HEDGES ON THE RIGHT, UNTIL SHORTLY AFTER IT BECOMES HEDGED ON BOTH SIDES. HERE THE 'WAYMARKED FIELD PATH' 350 YARDS ALONG THE COUNTY ROAD IN NEWNHAM, STARTS ON THE RIGHT.

The main route turns left, past Aston Holdings, and at the T-junction continues into the field ahead, soon veering left to follow a field-edge path under telephone lines that leads to Wood Lane. Here we turn right along the lane for 750 yards, where a sign-

WALK 6
WILMCOTE & ASTON CANTLOW

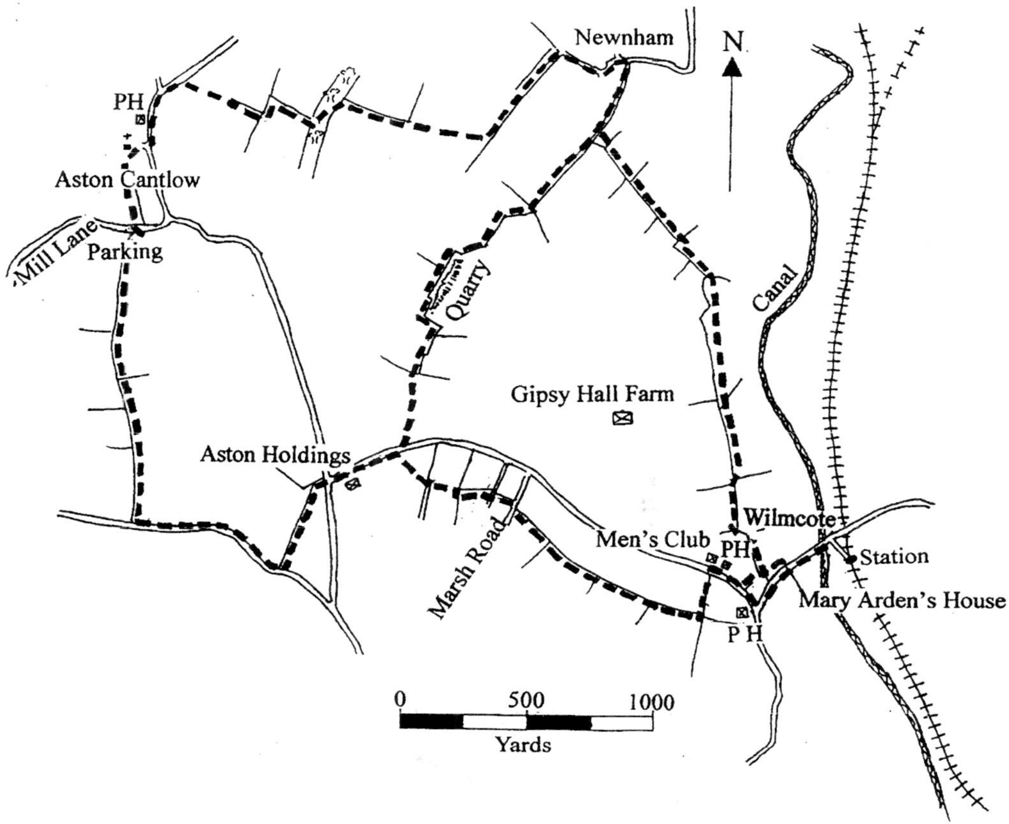

posted path on the right follows a rabbit-infested hedge for ¾ mile. It crosses Mill Lane at a point where the wide verges seem suitable for car parking. (To reach this point by road, turn right at the T-junction just to the south of Aston Cantlow; it is just 200 yards along the lane).

Our route heads towards the church, crossing a bridge and going through the churchyard. The church of St John the Baptist (mainly late 13th century) has some interesting features, and it is reputed that Shakespeare's parents were married there. In 2000, it received national publicity when the owners of a nearby field were judged to be responsible for meeting the costs of repairs to the chancel.

We pass – or visit – the Kings Head and continue round the bend in Bearley Road to the end of the row of bungalows on the right. Here a track heads across arable land, going clockwise round two sides of the second field, before climbing back up to the Wilmcote plateau. The track is in fact a county road, and use by horses and motor vehicles makes the steep incline very muddy at times; a minor detour through the bushes may help.

At the top, there are again good views. After a gateway, the track continues alongside a hedge on the left before crossing an open field. We turn left at the next hedgeline and follow the track (now a bridleway) into the hamlet of Newnham, with some nicely-restored properties.

After the grassy triangle with a pole on it, we turn right down another county road – we guess that these roads were once an important part of the infrastructure of the stone quarries in the area. After 350 yards, a waymarked field path starts on the left. (This is the point where the short cut rejoins the main route). After a bridge in the field corner, keep hedges on your right through a succession of five fields. During most of the nineteenth century it would not have been so peaceful in the area beyond those hedges, as the face of the stone quarry advanced towards Newnham; there were lime-burning kilns, and a railway

to transport the stone products to the canal at Wilmcote. Look in the far corner of the fifth field for traces of the old railway, curving round on a slight embankment.

A few more stiles bring you to the paddock at the rear of Mary Arden's House, and maybe a short cut to the back of the Masons Arms pub. The path ends opposite the Post Office Stores, where you turn left for the station or right to return to Aston Cantlow.

PLEASE RESPECT THE COUNTRYSIDE

While walkers have a right to use public paths, they also have a responsibility to ensure that they do not damage the environment or disrupt the activities of those who live and work in the countryside.

If you have a dog, please keep it under control at all times, and remember that it is illegal to allow a dog to be at large in a field in which there are sheep.

Please do not assume that the places that we suggest for car parking can accommodate more than one or two cars.

CLOTHING AND FOOTWEAR

Although 'wellies' and an umbrella may not be *de rigueur*, there may be times when their use will enable you to finish a walk in a more comfortable state than your more conventionally-clad companions! But on most occasions comfortable clothing adequate for the predicted weather conditions, and a pair of boots or stout shoes, should suffice.

REFRESHMENTS

All our main walks are served by at least one public house that provides lunchtime meals. At the time of writing, most offer a predictable menu of good and moderately-priced food. There is a trend towards the conversion of country pubs to more up-market restaurants, and we suggest that the Crab Mill at Preston Bagot and the King's Head at Aston Cantlow now come into this category.

Please remember to take a change of footwear if you are visiting any eating place during a walk. Even in dry weather, it is a gesture that the management will appreciate.